Lightning Bolt Books™

Alligators
Wetland Engineers

Heather E. Schwartz

Lerner Publications ◆ Minneapolis

Lerner Publications Company
An imprint of Lerner Publishing Group, Inc.
241 First Avenue North
Minneapolis, MN 55401 USA

For reading levels and more information, look up this title at www.lernerbooks.com.

Main body text set in Billy Infant Regular. Typeface provided by SparkyType.

Editor: Brianna Kaiser **Designer:** Martha Kranes **Photo Editor:** Lucien Brinkley

Library of Congress Cataloging-in-Publication Data

Names: Schwartz, Heather E., author.
Title: Alligators : wetland engineers / Heather E. Schwartz.
Description: Minneapolis : Lerner Publications , [2025] | Series: Lightning bolt books. Ecosystem engineers | Includes bibliographical references and index. | Audience: Ages 6-9 | Audience: Grades 2-3 | Summary: "Alligators are engineers of the wetlands. Readers will learn all about these amazing animals, including where they live, their life cycle, how they change their environment, and how the changes they make benefit other wildlife"— Provided by publisher.
Identifiers: LCCN 2024008812 (print) | LCCN 2024008813 (ebook) | ISBN 9798765647608 (library binding) | ISBN 9798765662014 (paperback) | ISBN 9798765655795 (epub)
Subjects: LCSH: Alligators—Juvenile literature. | Alligators—Ecology—Juvenile literature. | Alligators—Life cycles—Juvenile literature.
Classification: LCC QL666.C925 S345 2025 (print) | LCC QL666.C925 (ebook) | DDC 597.98/4—dc23/eng/20240320

LC record available at https://lccn.loc.gov/2024008812
LC ebook record available at https://lccn.loc.gov/2024008813

Manufactured in the United States of America
1-1010836-53321-4/4/2024

Table of Contents

Making Change

An alligator pushes its snout into the wet ground. It digs with its claws. It moves mud with its long, strong tail.

The alligator is making a hole where it will rest. The hole will fill with water from the ground. Other animals that need water will also use the hole.

The alligator and the other animals are part of the same wetland ecosystem. An ecosystem is an area where plants, animals, and everything around them work together.

Wetlands are areas of land that are covered with water most of the time.

An alligator hole

When alligators dig holes, they change their ecosystem.

That makes them ecosystem engineers.

Digging Holes

Alligators live in the southeastern United States. They spend most of their time in bodies of fresh water such as rivers, ponds, and lakes.

There is less water during the months when the weather is dry and warm. Alligators dig holes that fill with water and keep them cool.

During colder months, some alligators sink into the mud at the bottom of fresh water. The mud keeps the alligators warm.

Alligators can't make their own body heat, so they use their surroundings for heat.

Alligators use their claws, tails, and snouts to dig holes and tunnels.

Other alligators dig holes or tunnels in mud. The alligators rest, sleep, and stay warm in

Helping Animals and Plants

Alligators dig holes to help them live. Those holes also help plants and other animals.

Alligators share ecosystems with many animals such as fish, birds, and turtles. Those animals use the alligator holes for water during dry weather.

Mud sometimes starts to fill the alligator holes. Alligators use their snouts, claws, and tails to keep the mud out.

When alligators dig their holes, they move soil around. The soil has nutrients plants need to grow. New plants grow around the holes.

Plants grow around this alligator hole.

Lives of Alligators

After mating, a female alligator builds a nest on land near fresh water. The nest is made of mud, sticks, and plants. The female alligator lays her eggs in the nest.

About sixty-five days later, the eggs hatch. The hatchlings are only about the length of a pencil. But they can already swim and hunt.

Young alligators grow each year. Adult female alligators are about 8 feet (2.4 m) long or longer. Adult male alligators can be up to 15 feet (4.6 m) long.

The adult alligators will one day have their own hatchlings. The young alligators will grow, dig holes, and become new ecosystem engineers.

Two hatchlings rest on their mother.

Draw an Alligator Hole

The holes alligators make help the alligators, plants, and other animals. On a sheet of paper, draw a hole. Add an alligator and other animals that can use the hole.

Alligator Facts

- **Adult weight:** 200 pounds (91 kg) or more for females; about 500 to 1,000 pounds (227 to 454 kg) for males
- **Diet:** fish, turtles, snakes, small mammals, and birds
- **Group name:** congregation
- **Life span:** about thirty to fifty years

Glossary

ecosystem: an area where plants, animals, and everything around them live and work together

ecosystem engineer: a living thing such as an animal that changes its ecosystem with its actions

fresh water: water that is not salty

hatchling: a baby alligator

mating: two animals joining to create offspring, or babies

nutrient: a part of food that helps animals and plants grow

snout: the front part of an alligator's head, including the mouth and nose

wetland: an area of land often covered with water, such as a swamp or marsh

Learn More

Britannica Kids: Alligator
https://kids.britannica.com/kids/article/alligator/352737

Feldman, Thea. *Alligators and Crocodiles Can't Chew! And Other Amazing Facts.* New York: Simon Spotlight, 2021.

Gish, Melissa. *Alligator.* Mankato, MN: Creative Education, 2021.

National Geographic Kids: American Alligator
https://kids.nationalgeographic.com/animals/reptiles/facts/american-alligator

Schwartz, Heather E. *Beavers: Freshwater Engineers.* Minneapolis: Lerner Publications, 2025.

Smithsonian's National Zoo & Conservation Biology Institute: American Alligator
https://nationalzoo.si.edu/animals/american-alligator

Index

Photo Acknowledgments

Image credits: viktor2013/Getty Images, p. 4; Michael Patrick O'Neill/Alamy, p. 5; Diana Robinson Photography/Getty Images, p. 6; cturtletrax/Getty Images, p. 7; Dennis W Donohue/Shutterstock, p. 8; tsmarkley/Getty Images, p. 9; Robert Belbin/Alamy, p. 10; 6381380/Getty Images, p. 11; Holcy/Getty Images, p. 12; Jeff R Clow/Getty Images, p. 13; blickwinkel/Alamy, p. 14; © Pete Oxford/Minden Pictures, p. 15; Everglades National Park, p. 16; George Shelley/Getty Images, p. 17; Troy Harrison/Getty Images, pp. 18-19; trait2lumiere/Getty Images, p. 20.

Cover image: Michael S. Nolan/Alamy.